ASMA' BINT ABI BAKR

may Allah be pleased with her

by
Ahmad Thomson

Ta-Ha Publishers Ltd
1 Wynne Road
London SW9 0BB

© Safar 1414/July 1993 Ta-Ha Publishers

Published by

Ta-Ha Publishers Ltd
1 Wynne Road
London SW9 0BB

Editing and typesetting by Bookwork, Slough

British Library Cataloguing in Publication Data
Thomson, Ahmad
Asma' bint Abi Bakr, may Allah be pleased with her
1. Islam
I. Title

ISBN 1 897940 05 X

Printed by: Deluxe Printers, London. Tel: 081-965-1771

Contents

بسم الله الرحمن الرحيم

INTRODUCTION

What is there that a woman may not do? She can do everything except what Allah has forbidden. The teachings of Islam tell us what the limits of behaviour are. Anyone who goes beyond these limits is likely to meet trouble, both in this world and in the next world.

The best of women have lived their lives within the limits of Allah and have achieved greatness, often through actions which even the best of men could not have equalled. They have gained the love and respect not only of those who knew them, but also of those who came to hear about them long after they had died.

Among the best of women were the wives of the Prophet Muhammad, may the blessings and peace of Allah be on him and on his family and Companions, for he, may Allah bless him and grant him peace, was the best of creation, *Al-Quthum*, the one who has all good virtues and characteristics gathered together in him, and accordingly Allah granted him the best of women in marriage.

And among the best of women were the daughters of the Prophet Muhammad, may Allah bless him and grant him peace, for they had the best of parents, may Allah bless them and grant them peace.

And among the best of women were those who accepted Allah and His Messenger during his lifetime, may the blessings and peace of Allah be on him and on his family and on his companions, who learned from him and acted on what they knew. One of these women was Asma' bint Abi Bakr, may Allah be pleased with her, who was the daughter of *Sayyiduna* Abu Bakr as-Siddiq, may Allah be pleased with him.

Today, even hundreds of years later, young girls still learn a little about women such as these, and then, as they grow up and become women themselves, they follow their example, seeking the pleasure of Allah.

This small book is for you, so that, *insh'Allah,* you will learn something that you did not know before.

It has been related by Qadi 'Iyad that Sahl ibn 'Abdullah at-Tustari said, "Anyone who does not respect the Messenger's Companions nor esteem his commands does not believe in him," and that 'Abdullah ibn al-Mubarak said, "There are two qualities which are the cause of salvation for whoever has them: truthfulness and love for the Companions of Muhammad."

ASMA' BINT ABI BAKR

may Allah be pleased with her

Asma', may Allah be pleased with her, was the eldest daughter of *Sayyiduna* Abu Bakr رضه and the elder half-sister of A'isha رضه. She, like her father, was one of the first people to embrace Islam. Only seventeen people accepted Islam before her, so in her long life that spanned a hundred years, she experienced the extraordinary growth of the Muslim community, right from the very early days, when each member of that community knew and trusted each other completely, up to the death of the Prophet, may Allah bless him and grant him peace, through the time of the four Rightly-guided Khalifs, may Allah be pleased with them, and into the time when civil discord disturbed the peace of the Muslim community, as those who were hungry for power tried to take over from those whose only hunger was for knowledge of Allah and doing what is pleasing to Him. What a life she must have had!

Like Fatima az-Zahra', the daughter of the Prophet Muhammad ﷺ , Asma' personally witnessed many of the incidents, both the good and the bad, that occurred in Makka during the early years of Islam, and like Fatima she endured the three year exile that the Muslims spent in the small ravine outside Makka. Asma' was older than Fatima, however, so her understanding of events was probably different.

Since her father, Abu Bakr رضه, was the closest Companion of the Prophet صلعم, Asma' was often aware of exactly what was going on, as soon as it happened. When the time came for the Prophet to make *hijra* to

Madina, for example, Asma' was one of the few people who knew what the Prophet's plan was.

Indeed it was Asma' who used to slip out of Makka to bring the Prophet and her father food while they were hiding in the cave of Thawr, as long as the Quraysh continued to search for them. Her brother, 'Abdullah, also helped by listening to what the Quraysh were planning during the day, and then visiting the two men in the cave in the late afternoon to let them know what he had heard.

A man called Ibn Fuhayra, a slave whom Abu Bakr had set free and then given a job as a shepherd, would then drive his small flock of goats near the cave so that the Prophet and Abu Bakr could drink their fill of milk, and then, when he left, all that could be seen on the path to the cave were the hoof marks of Ibn Fuhayra's goats.

After three days, when the search had finally died down and the Quraysh had all but given up hope of finding their quarry, Asma' came to the cave with food for their long journey to Madina, while a guide came with three camels. Asma' could not find anything with which to tie the bags of food to their saddles, so she undid her waist wrapper, ripped it in two, put one half back on, and used the other half to secure the provisions for the journey. The Prophet ﷺ smiled at her ingenuity and said, *"Dhat an-Nitaqayn"* - "She of the two waist wrappers" - and this became her title for the rest of her long life.

When Abu Bakr رضي left Makka, he took what little wealth he had left with him, for although he had once been a very wealthy man, he had spent most of his money in the way of Allah during the thirteen years that the Messenger of Allah had spent calling on the people of Makka to abandon their life of ignorance and idol-worship, and to embrace Islam and worship only Allah.

When Abu Bakr's father, Abu Quhafa, who was old and blind and had not yet accepted Islam, heard that Abu Bakr had left, he came to visit Asma' and said, "I hear that Abu Bakr has abandoned you without leaving you any money?"

"Not at all," she replied, "come and feel for yourself." She guided his hand over to the small recess in the wall where Abu Bakr رضي normally kept his money, and which she had filled with some small pebbles, covered with a cloth. To him it felt like gold, and so Asma' managed to calm any fears that he may have had, as well as avoiding having to accept any money from him.

Zubayr, Asma's husband, who was in a caravan of merchants returning from Syria, met the Messenger of Allah and Abu Bakr on their way to Madina and gave them fresh white clothes. The people in Madina were waiting expectedly and every morning they went out to the lava-field to wait for him until the intense heat drove them back to Madina. One day after they had been waiting a very long time and had returned to their houses, a man climbed to the top of a fortress and suddenly saw them shimmering in white through the heat. He shouted, "The one who you have been waiting for is coming!" The Muslims rushed out to meet them.

After the Prophet and Abu Bakr had safely reached Madina, where they were welcomed with much rejoicing, those Muslims who still remained in Makka also made *hijra* to Madina as soon as they were able. This was an extraordinary time for the early Muslims, when they were few in number, when they were opposed by countless *kafirun*, and when it sometimes seemed as if each day might indeed be their last. And yet these were glorious days, both for those who made *hijra* from Makka - the Muhajirun, and for those in Madina who welcomed them - the Ansar, may Allah be pleased with all of them. Allah says of these people:

The forerunners, the first of the Muhajirun
and the Ansar,
and those who have followed them in doing good,

**Allah is pleased with them
and they are pleased with Him.
He has made ready for them Gardens
with rivers flowing under them,
in them timelessly forever without end.
That is the Great Victory.**
(Qur'an: 9.100)

Gradually the Muslims who remained in Makka left the city and travelled to Madina to join their beloved Prophet. Amongst them was Asma', who travelled with the members of the families of the Prophet Muhammad and Abu Bakr, may Allah bless them and grant them peace. The party included Umm Kulthum, Fatima, Sawda, Zayd ibn Haritha, Baraka, Usama ibn Zayd, Abu Bakr's present wife (Asma's own mother, Qutayla, had been divorced even before the revelation of the Qur'an had begun), his son 'Abdullah and his other daughter, 'A'isha, who would soon be marrying the Prophet and becoming a part of his household, may the blessings and peace of Allah be on him and on his family and Companions.

The journey was not an easy one for Asma', for she was very pregnant - but she did it, and when they reached Quba, on the outskirts of Madina, she gave birth to a son. He was the first baby to be born into Islam after the *hijra*, and so his birth was perhaps celebrated even more than usual, for he was a new life in a new place, a new beginning.

The small baby was taken to the Prophet Muhammad صلعم, who put him on his lap and asked for some dates to be brought. When, after a while, some dates had been found, the Prophet chewed them first and then put some of his saliva into the baby's mouth. This was the first thing to enter his stomach. It is related by Asma' that the Prophet then rubbed his palate with the chewed up dates, and asked Allah to bless him, and gave him the name of 'Abdullah. She continues:

"He ('Abdullah ibn Zubayr) went to him (the Prophet صلى الله عليه وسلم), when he had reached the age of seven or eight years in order to pledge his allegiance to the Messenger of Allah صلى الله عليه وسلم, as Zubayr had commanded him to do. The Messenger of Allah صلى الله عليه وسلم smiled when he saw him coming towards him and then accepted his allegiance."

Like many of the Muhajirun during the early years in Madina, Asma' was both very poor and very generous, for she understood the words of the Prophet صلى الله عليه وسلم, "Whoever does not prefer giving to receiving has not tasted the sweetness of poverty", and she knew that as long as she worshipped and praised Allah, then she would be clothed and sheltered and fed.

'Abdullah ibn Zubayr once said of Asma' and her half-sister 'A'isha, "I have not seen two women more generous than my aunt 'A'isha and my mother Asma' - but their generosity was expressed in different ways: My aunt would gather one thing after another together, until she had collected what she thought was enough, and then she would distribute it all to those who were in need. My mother, on the other hand, would not keep anything, even for the next day."

ZUBAYR IBN AL-'AWWAM,
the husband of Asma'

Asma' was married to a man named Zubayr ibn al-'Awwam, who also embraced Islam very early on, shortly after Abu Bakr رضه, at the age of fifteen or sixteen. Zubayr was in fact a cousin of the Prophet, and in the ripeness of time proved to be one of the most valiant and fearless Companions of the Prophet, may the blessings and peace of Allah be on him and his family and Companions. Indeed, he was the first Muslim to unsheathe a sword in the Way of Allah.

The Prophet صلعم once said of Zubayr, "Surely every Prophet has a helper, and my helper is Zubayr." The Prophet صلعم also said of Zubayr, "Zubayr ibn al-'Awwam is one of the pillars of Islam."

Although Asma's husband, Zubayr ibn al-'Awwam, eventually became one of the richest Muslims in Madina, he and his family had virtually nothing when they first arrived in Madina. It has been related by Asma' that to begin with, they had no land, no wealth, and no servants. All that Zubayr possessed was a horse and a camel, which Asma' used to look after for him.

She said, "I grazed his horse, provided fodder for it, and looked after it, as well as grinding date-stones for his camel. Besides this, I grazed the camel, provided it with water, patched our leather bucket, and kneaded the flour. I was not very good at baking bread, so my neighbours used to bake the bread for me, for they were sincere women."

"Once," said Asma', "I was carrying a load of date-stones on my head from the land of Zubayr which the Messenger of Allah صلعم which was about two miles away. As I was walking along with the date-stones on my head, I happened to meet the Messenger of Allah ﷺ who was with a group of his Companions. He called out to me, and told his camel to kneel down so that I could ride behind him."

Asma', however, refused the offer and later told her husband, "I felt shy to do so, and thought that you might be jealous."

"By Allah," replied Zubayr, "The thought of your having to carry the date-stones on your head is far more troubling to me than your riding behind him ﷺ."

Zubayr and Asma' continued to lead a difficult life until Abu Bakr رض gave them a maid servant as a present who then looked after the horse for Asma'.

"I felt as if I had been set free," said Asma', "for nothing had been more of a burden to me than looking after the horse."

Some time after this, a poor man came to Asma's door and said, "O Umm 'Abdullah, I am destitute and I would like to start a business in the shadow of your house."

"If I give you permission," replied Asma', "Zubayr may not agree to that, so you should come and ask again when Zubayr is also here."

Accordingly, the poor man waited until Zubayr was at home, and then again asked, "O Umm 'Abdullah, I am destitute and I would like to start a business in the shadow of your house."

"Isn't there anywhere else in Madina except my house?" she replied.

"Why do you want to stop this poor man starting his business here?" exclaimed Zubayr.

And so the poor man set up his business outside their house and made so much money that one day they sold their maid servant to him. Zubayr came into the room when Asma' had the money in her lap and asked her to give it to him, but she replied, "No, I intend to give it away as *sadaqa*."

It has been related by Asma' that she once went to the Prophet ﷺ and said, "O Messenger of Allah, I have nothing other than what Zubayr gives me. Is there anything wrong in my giving away some of what has been given to me?"

"Spend according to your means," the Prophet replied, " and do not calculate, or Allah will calculate with you; and do not hoard, or Allah will withold from you."

It is clear that Asma' was a sensitive woman who honoured her husband, but they did not always see eye to eye.

On one occasion she went to her father to complain about the way Zubayr was treating her. "My daughter, be patient," replied Abu Bakr, "for if a woman has a righteous husband and he dies and she does not marry after him, then they will be re-united in the Garden."

Zubayr ﷺ was certainly a righteous man, and one of the nine men with whom the Prophet said that he was well-pleased shortly before his death - and accordingly one of the six men from whom 'Umar ﷺ indicated that his own successor should be chosen.

Zubayr was also one of the ten Companions who were told by the Prophet ﷺ that they would be in the Garden. He was a man who lived his life completely in the way of Allah, and accordingly he was very scrupulous in his behaviour, towards people and towards Allah.

Zubayr was one of the most fearless warriors among the Companions. He received one of his three wounds at Badr, and he took 'Abdullah, who was ten years old, with him on his horse, to accustom him to battle.

After the battle of Uhud when the Prophet feared that the idol-worshippers might return, he selected seventy men to go after them. These men included Abu Bakr and Zubayr ﷺ. 'A'isha spoke about these verses of the Qur'an:

**Of those who answered
the call of Allah and the Messenger,
even after being wounded,
those who do right and refrain from wrong
have a great reward**

(3:172)

She said to 'Urwa ibn az-Zubayr, "My nephew, your fathers, az-Zubayr and Abu Bakr, were among them on the day on Uhud when the Messenger of Allah ﷺ was afflicted by what he was afflicted. The idolworshippers left him and he feared that he might return and said, 'Who will go after them?' He selected seventy men from them. Abu Bakr and az-Zubayr were among them.'"

'Urwa said, "Az-Zubayr had three sword scars: one was on his shoulder. I used to put my fingers into it. He got two blows in the Battle of Badr and one in the Battle of Yarmuk." '

'Urwa then spoke about the Battle of Yarmuk where the Byzantines were defeated, "The Companions of the Messenger of Allah said to az-Zubayr on day of the Battle of Yarmuk, 'Will you attack and we will attack with you?' He said, 'If I attack, you will fail to attack.' They said, 'We will not do that.' So he attacked them until he pierced through their lines and went beyond them and no one was with him. Then he turned to return and they grabbed his rein and struck him two blows on his shoulder between which was the blow he had received at the Battle of Badr.'"

'Urwa added, "I used to put my fingers in those scars while playing when I was a child."

Zubayr also carried the Prophet's banner when Makka was conquered.

On one occasion, on the Prophet's Farewell Pilgrimage, in 10 AH, Asma' was permitted to take off her *ihram* after they had reached Makka and performed

the *'umra* - before putting on *ihram* again for the actual
rites of the *hajj* - because she did not have an animal to
sacrifice. Zubayr, on the other hand, had brought a sacri-
ficial animal with him, and accordingly he remained in
the same *ihram* for both the *'umra* and the *hajj*.

When Asma' had changed into ordinary clothes, she
came out and sat next to Zubayr, who immediately said,
"Keep away from me! Keep away from me!" for he did
not want anything to happen that might break his *ihram*.
Whereupon Asma' replied a little lightly, "Why? Are you
afraid that I'm going to jump on you?"

It has been related by 'Abdullah, the freed slave of
Asma', that whenever Asma' passed by a place called
Hajun, she would recall the Prophet's Farewell Pilgrim-
age - which had been the first of her many *hajjs* - and say,
"May the blessings and peace of Allah be on His
Messenger. We used to stay here along with him, with
light burdens. Few were our mounts, and scarce were our
provisions."

One day the Prophet صلى الله عليه وسلم was asleep and Zubayr sat
down and kept the flies away from his face. Then the
Prophet woke up and said to him, "Jibril greets you and
says, 'I will be with you on the Day of Rising so that I
can drive away the sparks of the Fire of Jahannam from
your face.'"

In later years, when Zubayr رضي الله عنه became a wealthy
man, Asma' still continued to lead a simple life. Once,
when another son of hers, al-Mundhir, sent her a fancy
dress from Iraq, she felt its fine fabric - for like her
grandfather before her, she had gone blind - and told
whoever had brought it to send it back.

Al-Mundhir was upset by this and pointed out that the
material was not transparent. "It may not be transparent,"
replied his mother, "but it is tight-fitting and shows the
shape of my body." So al-Mundhir chose a more sensible
dress for her, and this time she accepted it.

After the peace treaty of Hudaybiyya between the Muslims and the Quraysh had been signed, in 6 AH, Asma's mother, Qutayla, came to Madina to visit her daughter. Asma' was not sure how to treat her at first, because although her mother was not opposed to the Muslims, she had not accepted Islam. To begin with, Asma' would not let her mother enter her house, and refused to accept the gifts that she had brought for her daughter. Instead Asma' sent someone to 'A'isha to ask the Prophet ﷺ what she should do.

The Prophet ﷺ replied that Asma' should welcome her mother into her house and accept her gifts, and it was in these circumstances that the following *ayats* of the Qur'an were revealed:

**Allah does not forbid you
from being kind and just
towards those
who did not make war on you
because of your *deen*
or drive you from your homes.
Surely Allah loves those who are just.**

**Surely Allah only forbids you
from making friends with those
who made war on you because of your *deen* and drove
you from your homes and helped to drive you away.
And whoever makes friends with them,
they are indeed wrong-doers.**

(Qur'an: 60.8-9)

Like many of the women of Madina, Asma' رضه spent much of her time in prayer and fasting and remembering Allah. This was what made her heart peaceful, and these were the actions of the people whose company she kept, the company of the Prophet Muhammad, may the blessings and peace of Allah be on him and on his family and on his Companions.

Like 'Ali and Fatima az-Zahra', may Allah bless them and grant them peace, Zubayr ibn al-'Awwam and Asma' loved Allah and His Messenger صلى, and they fought and struggled in the way of Allah, both before and after his death, may his grave be filled with peace and light.

They had both accepted Islam at the very beginning of the affair, and together they had witnessed the extraordinary growth and flowering of the first Muslim community that had sprung up around and been inspired by their beloved Prophet صلى. They had several sons including 'Abdullah, 'Urwa and Mus'ab, and they liked to name them after those martyred in the way of Allah.

THE GREAT FITNA

After the Prophet's death, they experienced the time of the four Rightly guided Khalifs - Abu Bakr, 'Umar, 'Uthman, and 'Ali - the last three of whom were all murdered, may Allah be pleased with them - during which the territorial boundaries of the Muslim *Ummah* expanded rapidly. It was during this period, which spanned the first forty years after the Prophet's death صلعم, that the signs of discord which the Prophet himself had predicted, began to appear more openly, especially after the death of 'Umar ibn al-Khattab.

Once when 'Uthman ibn 'Affan was khalif and was afflicted with such a severe nose-bleed that he was prevented from going on *hajj*, he made a will. A man of the Quraysh visited him and said, "Appoint a successor." He said, "They have said that?" He said, "Yes." He said, "Who?' He was silent. He said, "Perhaps they said az-Zubayr?" He said, 'Yes.' He said, 'By the One in whose hand my soul is, he is the best of them as far as I know and he was the most beloved of them to the Messenger of Allah." Another reported that he said, "By Allah, you know that he is the best of you," three times.

Things reached such a pitch that 'Uthman رضه was beseiged in his house by rebels and dissidents who had come from Egypt

While Zubayr was trying to rally assistance for the denfence of the Khalif, his son, 'Abdullah, was one of those in the house who were defending 'Uthman رضه. The defenders included al-Hasan ibn 'Ali, 'Abdullah ibn 'Umar, Abu Hurayra. Sa'id ibn al-'As and Marwan ibn al-Hakam. 'Uthman, however, did not want to be responsible for shedding Muslim blood and sent them away. 'Abdullah ibn Zubayr was the last to leave, only doing so with great reluctance.

It was during the unfortunate Battle of the Camel, which took place after the murder of 'Uthman رضه and in which two armies of Muslims - one led by 'Ali and the other led by 'A'isha, Zubayr and Talha - somehow suddenly found themselves facing each other, that Zubayr رضه was murdered.

When Zubayr and 'Ali met and spoke about the situation, Zubayr left, not wanting to fight other Muslims. Some of the murderers of 'Uthman followed him and then murdered him. His death was just one of many of the unfortunate incidents that were a result of the general confusion and misunderstanding that surrounded this event, which took place in 36 AH, only twenty-five years after the Prophet's death, may Allah bless him and grant him peace.

Perhaps recalling the advice that her father had given her many years previously, Asma' did not remarry. With her clear memories of all that had taken place in her lifetime so far, she continued to remember and worship Allah constantly and to witness what was happening to the Muslim *Ummah*.

The discord that had claimed her husband's life grew worse - especially after the murder of 'Ali - as the old tribal rivalry and feuding that the Prophet صلعم had done so much to dispel, may Allah bless him and grant him peace, began to clearly re-emerge, and the power struggles - not only between those who merely wanted power, but also between those who wanted power and those who seriously and sincerely wanted to uphold the *deen* of Islam in its original form - became ever more intense. There were also intense disagreements over who should be the ruler and how things should be done.

Even today, this period of history is a painful one for Muslims to explore. It is not always easy to see what happened and why it happened. It is so important not to form a false picture of what took place, or to jump to wrong conclusions, or to pass judgement blindly without knowledge, or to think or speak badly of any of the Companions of the Prophet Muhammad, may the blessings and peace of Allah be on him and on his family and Companions, that some Muslims prefer not to look at it at all.

Those who know the most about this time often say, "We were not there; we were not part of it," and remain silent. It is better and safer to weep, for in tears there is knowledge and humility and acceptance - acceptance that Allah has power over all things and that He does what He wants with His creation.

When one of the great Tabi'un, ar-Rabi' ibn Khaytham, heard that al-Husayn, the Prophet's grandson, had been killed, all that he said was, "O Allah, Creator of the heavens and the earth, Knower of the Unseen and the Visible! You will judge between Your slaves regarding that about which they disagree!"

This is something that Asma' رضه must have known for having lost her beloved husband in the *Fitna,* she also lost two of her three sons, 'Abdullah ibn Zubayr, the first person to be born into Islam after the *hijra*, and Mus'ab ibn Zubayr.

After the death of Mu'awiya ibn Abi Sufyan, who became the khalif after 'Ali رضه, came the rule of Yazid ibn Mu'awiya, who was considered by some parties to be responsible for the martyrdom of Husayn رضه.

After Yazid's death, 'Abdullah ibn Zubayr was acclaimed as the new khalif by some of the Muslims, particularly in the Hijaz. Mus'ab was appointed as his brother's lieutenant in Iraq.

However, the descendants of Mu'awiya, who became known as the Umayyads from their family name, the Banu Umayya, considered that the khalifate should remain within their family in order to ensure continuity of rule and the expansion of Islam, and they fought

'Abdullah ibn Zubayr and the various groups of rebels
that sprang up relentlessly to this end.

In 63 AH 'Abdullah ibn Zubayr, who had refused to
pledge allegiance to Yazid, was forced to take refuge in
the sanctuary of the Ka'ba. The commander of the
Umayyad army, al-Husayn ibn Numayr, besieged Makka,
surrounding the city and catapulting it with large stones,
in spite of the well-known fact that on the day of the conquest of Makka, in 8 AH, the Prophet صلعم said:

"Allah made this city sacred on the day that He creat-
ed the earth and the heavens, so it is sacred by the sacredness conferred on it by Allah until the Day of Resur-rec-
tion. Fighting in it was not permitted to anyone before
me, and it was permitted for me only during one hour on
one day, for it is sacred by the sacredness conferred on it
by Allah until the Day of Resurrection."

It has been related by Abu Shurayh al-'Adawi that he
said to 'Amr ibn Sa'id, who was one of the commanders
of the army besieging Makka, "Let me tell you something, O commander, which the Messenger of Allah صلعم
said on the day following the conquest which my ears
heard and my heart has retained, and my eyes saw as he
spoke it. He praised Allah and glorified Him and then he
said, 'Allah, not people, has made Makka sacred, so it is
not permitted for any person who believes in Allah and
the Last Day to shed blood in it, or cut down a tree in it.
If anyone seeks an excuse based on the fighting of the
Messenger of Allah, then tell him that Allah permitted
His Messenger, but not you, and He gave him permission
only for one hour on one day, and then its sacredness was
restored on the same day to what it had been the day
before. Let whoever is present convey this information to
whomever is absent.'"

'Amr ibn Sa'id, who was not one of the Companions
of the Prophet صلعم, replied, "I know about that better
than you do, Abu Shurayh, but the sanctuary does not

grant protection to whoever is disobedient, or to whoever runs away after shedding blood, or to whoever runs away after committing a crime."

This reply of 'Amr ibn Sa'id summed up both Yazid's accusation against 'Abdullah ibn Zubayr and his justification for besieging him in Makka - but many of the Muslims felt that the fault lay with Yazid, whom they accused of drinking wine and not praying, an allegation for which they had no witnesses. Indeed, 'Ali's son, Muhammad ibn al-Hanafiyya, said that he had stayed with Yazid and seen him constantly in prayer and asking about the *sunna*.

Part of the confusion and discord of the time is indicated by the fact that accusations and counter-accusations were flying in all directions, inflaming an already difficult situation. In the intensity of the moment, people had forgotten about having a good opinion of their fellow Muslims. Mu'awiya reported that the Messenger of Allah صلى said, "If you go about searching for the faults of Muslims, you will certainly corrupt them."

Eventually the Umayyad army withdrew from Makka, as a result of the confusion that followed the death of Yazid, but only after the Ka'ba had been severely damaged and partially destroyed by fire.

Accordingly 'Abdullah ibn Zubayr set about re-building the Ka'ba, and since he recalled that 'A'isha رضه had told him that the Prophet صلى had said to her after the conquest of Makka that he would have liked to have rebuilt the Ka'ba on the original foundations that had been used by the Prophet Ibrahim, peace be on him - 'Abdullah ibn Zubayr did exactly this. The *Hijr* was included in the building and two doors were made at ground level, the eastern one being used as an entrance and the western one being used as an exit.

It has been related by 'Abdullah ibn Zubayr that the Prophet صلى said, when talking of his mosque in

Madina, "Prayer in this mosque of mine is more excellent than a thousand prayers observed in other mosques, except al-Masjid al-Haram [at the Ka'ba] - and the prayer in al-Masjid al-Haram is as excellent as a hundred prayers done in this mosque."

The work done by 'Abdullah ibn Zubayr was not destined to last for long. In 73 AH, 'Abdullah ibn Zubayr was once again besieged in Makka by an even larger Umayyad army, led this time by al-Hajjaj ibn Yusuf ath-Thaqafi, the general of the army of 'Abdul-Malik ibn Marwan.

Initially, following 'Abdal-Malik's instructions, al-Hajjaj lay siege to Ibn Zubayr in Makka, basing himself at Ta'if, outside of the Haram. When it proved impossible for the *hajj* to take place because of the unsettled situation and the split between the Muslims was allowing their enemies to thrive, Abdal-Malik was convinced by his advisors that force would have to be used to resolve the situation. He then permitted al-Hajjaj to storm only that new part of the Ka'ba which Ibn Zubayr had added, believing it to not be part of the Ka'ba.

Al-Hajjaj eventually conquered Makka by sheer force - how different it was to the peaceful conquest of Makka by the Prophet Muhammad صلى الله عليه وسلم - and one of the first things he did, on the instructions of 'Abdal-Malik ibn Marwan, the Umayyad khalif, was to again separate the *Hijr* from the Ka'ba and wall up the west door, so that the building was practically restored to its previous form.

It has been related by Muslim that Harith ibn 'Abdullah subsequently led a delegation to 'Abdal-Malik ibn Marwan who was now recognised as the khalif by all the Muslims, and who said that he did not think that 'Abdullah ibn Zubayr had heard what he had said that he had heard from 'A'isha regarding the original form of the Ka'ba.

Harith replied that he himself had heard exactly the same thing from 'A'isha, and 'Abdul-Malik asked him what she had said. Harith's answer was this:

"She said that the Messenger of Allah ﷺ said, 'Truly your people have reduced the area of the House from its original foundations, and if they had not only recently abandoned idol-worship, I would have rebuilt what they have left out, and if your people take the initiative in rebuilding it after me, then come with me and I will show you what they have left out.' And he indicated to her about fifteen cubits from the side of the *Hatim* [the curved wall that borders the Hijr].

"The Messenger of Allah ﷺ also said, 'I would also make two doors at ground level, facing east and west. Do you know why your people raised the level of its door?'

"'No,' she said.

"'It was out of arrogance, so that they could allow entry only to whomever they wished. When a person intended to enter it, they would let him climb up and as he was about to go in, they would push him so that he fell down.'"

'Abdul-Malik ibn Marwan said to Harith, "Did you yourself hear her saying this?"

"Yes," he replied.

And 'Abdul-Malik scratched the ground with his staff for some time and then said, "I wish I had left his (Ibn Zubayr's) work alone. If I had heard this before having it demolished, I would have left it in the state in which Ibn Zubayr had rebuilt it."

As well as destroying 'Abdullah ibn Zubayr's work, al-Hajjaj also destroyed 'Abdullah ibn Zubayr himself. It has been related that shortly before al-Hajjaj entered Makka, 'Abdullah ibn Zubayr went to visit his mother, Asma' bint Abi Bakr, who was now over one hundred years old - an old, blind, woman, who was still young at heart and whose inner sight was still keen. After

exchanging greetings, she asked him why he had come to
see her, and he replied that he had come to seek her
advice.

"Many of the people have deserted me out of fear of
al-Hajjaj," began 'Abdullah ibn Zubayr, "or because they
are tempted by what he is offering them. Even my chil-
dren and my family have left me. There is only a small
group of men still with me now, and however strong and
brave they are, they can only resist for a little while
longer. Messengers from the Banu Umayya are now talking with me, offering me whatever wealth I want as long
as I surrender my arms and swear allegiance to 'Abdul-
Malik ibn Marwan. What do you say?"

"O 'Abdullah," she replied, "it is your affair, and you
yourself know best. If you believe that you are right and
that you are defending the truth, then persevere and fight
on, just as those of your companions who have already
been killed showed perseverance. If, however, you desire
this world, then what a miserable wretch you are. You
will have destroyed yourself and your men all for nothing."

"Then I will be killed today without any doubt,"
answered 'Abdullah ibn Zubayr.

"That is better than surrendering to al-Hajjaj," she
replied.

"I am not afraid of death," he answered, "but I am
afraid they will mutilate my body."

"There is nothing after death that a man should fear,"
Asma' retorted. "Skinning a dead sheep does not cause it
any pain."

"What a blessed mother you are!" exclaimed
'Abdullah ibn Zubayr. "I came to you at this time to hear
what I have heard. Allah knows that I have not weakened
or given up. He is my witness that I have not fought out
of love for this world and its attractions, but only out of
anger for the sake of Allah, because His limits have been

broken. Here I am, going towards what is pleasing to you, so if I am killed, do not grieve for me and pray to Allah for me."

"I would only grieve for you," said Asma', "if you were to be killed fighting in a useless and unjust cause."

"Be assured that your son has never supported any cause that is unjust, nor done anything that is detestable, nor been unjust to any Muslim or *dhimmi*, and that there is nothing better in his sight than the pleasure of Allah, the Mighty, the Majestic. I am not saying this to justify myself. Allah knows that I have only said this to make your heart firm and steadfast."

"Praise is for Allah," replied Asma', "Who has made you act in accordance with what is both pleasing to Him and pleasing to me. Come close to me, my son, so that I can smell and feel your body, for this may be the last meeting that we have."

'Abdullah knelt before his blind mother, and she hugged and kissed his head and face and neck. Suddenly she withdrew her hands.

"What is this you are wearing?" she asked.

"It is my armour."

"That, my son, is not the dress of someone who desires martyrdom. Take it off. It will make your movements lighter and quicker. Wear a robe instead, so that if you are killed, your *'awra* will not be exposed."

This 'Abdullah ibn Zubayr did, and after Asma' had made a long *du'a* for him, he bade her farewell and returned to the *Haram* where he rushed into the thickest part of the battle and defended himself until he was killed. He was 72 years old. On the orders of al-Hajjaj, his body was strung up on some scaffolding for all to see and left to rot.

Three days after her son had been killed, Asma' was led to where his body was hanging, and although she could not see it, she observed, "The time has not yet

come for the rider to dismount from his horse," and
returned to her room.

It is related by Abu Nawfal that when 'Abdullah ibn
'Umar - who travelled at this time to Makka with the
intention of doing an *'umra* and the *hajj* - came to see
what al-Hajjaj had done, he stood in front of the dead
body of 'Abdullah ibn Zubayr (who had also been known
by his *kunya* of Abu Khubayb) as it hung there, and said
in a loud voice that everyone could hear:

"May there be peace on you, Abu Khubayb; may there
be peace on you, Abu Khubayb; may there be peace on
you, Abu Khubayb. By Allah, I used to forbid you from
this; by Allah, I used to forbid you from this; by Allah, I
used to forbid you from this. By Allah, as far as I know,
you were a man devoted to fasting and prayer who took
great care in strengthening family ties. By Allah, your
party has been called wicked, but it is indeed a good
one."

'Abdullah's brother Mus'ab had already been killed in
Iraq while fighting 'Abdu'l-Malik. A measure of the dis-
order of the time is found in the fact that 'Abdu'l-Malik
and Mus'ab had been close friends in Madina when they
were young. 'Abdu'l-Malik was keen to spare Mus'ab's
life in return for his allegiance but in vain. Then he was
keen to save the life of Mus'ab's son, 'Isa, but 'Isa fell in
the battle before his father fell at the age of thirty-six.

'Abdullah's brother, 'Urwa, hastened to 'Abdu'l-
Malik on behalf of his mother to ask to be given the body
for burial, a request which was immediately granted and
a strong rebuke was sent to al-Hajjaj for his inhumanity.
'Abdullah's body was prompty surrendered to Asma' for
burial.

'Abdu'l-Malik said to 'Urwa, "'Urwa! Do you recog-
nise the sword of az-Zubayr?" He said that he did and
Abdal-Malik asked, 'What marks does it have?" I said,
"It has a dent on its edge which happened in the Battle of

Badr." 'Abdal-Malik said, "You spoke the truth. They
have dents from clashing with the regiments." Then he
returned it to 'Urwa.

'Urwa, and his son, Hisham, became two of the major
scholars of Islam. He collected information for the biog-
raphy of the Prophet, especially his expeditions and
passed on immense knowledge.

'Urwa was called one of "the seven *fuqaha'* of
Madina," eventually dying in 94 AH at the age of about
72. Of him Ibn Shihab said, "I discovered 'Urwa to be an
ocean whose water could not be exhausted."

Al-Hajjaj issued an order that Abdullah ibn Zubayr's
mother be brought to him, but Asma' refused to come.
He again sent a messenger to her, saying that if she did
not come he would have her brought by force. Asma'
again refused, saying that they would have to drag her by
her hair before she would come. Finally al-Hajjaj put on
his shoes and, puffed up with pride and arrogance though
he was, he came to her.

What do you think of what I have done with the
enemy of Allah?" he asked, meaning her son - who had
first pledged his allegiance to the Prophet ﷺ when he
was only seven or eight years old, may Allah be pleased
with him.

Asma' was not intimidated in the least by al-Hajjaj -
who had never even met the Prophet ﷺ.

"You have destroyed him in this world," she said,
"and so through him your life in the next world has been
destroyed. I have heard that you used to call him 'Ibn
Dhat an-Nitaqayn' -'the son of the one with two waist
wrappers'. By Allah, I am indeed the one with two waist
wrappers. One is the one which I used to tie up the food
of the Messenger of Allah ﷺ and Abu Bakr, so that it
was out of reach of the animals; and as for the other waist
wrapper, that is the waist wrapper with which no woman
can do without!"

What a contrast there was between this meeting with al-Hajjaj and the last meeting she had experienced with her son, 'Abdullah ibn Zubayr; and what a difference there was between Asma's understanding of life and of Islam and that of the arrogant and ignorant man who now stood before her.

In the course of her long life, may Allah be pleased with her, Asma' had enjoyed the best and most exalted of company, and as a result she had never been blind to what people are capable of doing to each other, whether good or bad.

When she was young she had witnessed - as she saw what the *kafirun* were doing to the Muslims - how cruel people can be; within the Muslim community itself, she had experienced how compassionate people can be; now that she was old, she had again witnessed how cruel people can be - only this time the cruelty was being inflicted in the name of Islam by people who called themselves Muslims, on Muslims. Asma', however, was not deceived by words, and she perceived the meaning of actions, whether good or bad, even though she was blind.

"Truly," she continued, "the Messenger of Allah صلعم told us that a great liar and a great murderer would both be born in Thaqif. The liar we have already seen [al-Mukhtar ibn Abi Ubayd, who claimed to be the one appointed by the Mahdi to lead the people]; and as far as the murderer is concerned, I do not see who else it can be other than you."

Al-Hajjaj did not say anything in reply. He stood up and left the room. However powerful his army might be, he was no match for an old woman who was not afraid to speak the truth.

Ten days after the death of her son, at the age of 100, Asma' herself died and rejoined the ones she loved.

CONCLUSION

Qadi 'Iyad wrote:

"Part of respecting and obeying the Prophet ﷺ consists in respecting his Companions, obeying them, recognising what is due to them, following them, praising them, asking forgiveness for them, refraining from discussing their differences, showing enmity to those who are hostile towards them and shunning the misguidance of the Shi'a and the innovators and the reports of any historians or ignorant transmitters who detract from any of them. If there is something equivocal which is reported about them regarding the trials that took place between them, then adopt the best interpretation and look for the most correct way out of it since that is what they deserve. None of them should be mentioned in a bad manner nor are they to be rebuked for anything. Rather, we mention their good deeds, their virtues and their praiseworthy lives and are silent about anything else."

The Prophet ﷺ said, "When my Companions are mentioned, hold back." (At-Tabarani).

Allah says, **"Muhammad is the Messenger of Allah, and those who are with him are hard against the unbelievers, merciful to the believers ..."** (Qur'an: 48.29) and **"The outstrippers, the first of the Muhajirun and the Ansar,"** (Qur'an: 9,100) and **"Allah was pleased with the believers when they gave allegiance to you under the tree,"** (Qur'an: 48.18) and **"Men who were true to their contract with Allah."** (Qur'an: 33.23).

The Prophet ﷺ said, "My Companions are like stars. Whichever of them you follow, you will be guided." (Al-Bazzar).

Anas said that the Messenger of Allah ﷺ said, "The likeness of my Companions is like salt in the food. Food is not good without it." (Al-Bazzar).

He said, "Allah! Allah! My Companions! Do not make them targets after me! Whoever loves them loves them by my love. Whoever hates them hates them by my hatred. Whoever harms them harms me. Whoever harms me harms Allah. Whoever harms Allah is about to be seized." (Ibn Abi Hatim).

Abu Sa'id al-Khudri said that the Prophet ﷺ said, "Do not curse my Companions. If any of you were to spend the weight of Uhud in gold, it still would not reach the measure of one of them or even one-half of it." (Muslim).

He said, "Anyone who curses my Companions has the curse of Allah on him, and of the angels, and of all people. Allah will not accept any exchange or recompense from him." (Ad-Daylami and Abu Nu'aym).

He said in the *hadith* from Jabir, "Allah chose my Companions over everything else in existence except for the Prophets and the Messengers. He chose four of them for me; Abu Bakr, 'Umar, 'Uthman and 'Ali. He made them my best Companions, and all of my Companions are good." (Al-Bazzar and ad-Daylami).

Qadi 'Iyad also wrote:

Ayyub as-Sakhtiyani said, "Whoever loves Abu Bakr has established the *deen*. Whoever loves 'Umar has made the way clear. Whoever loves 'Uthman has been illuminated by the light of Allah. Whoever loves 'Ali has taken hold of the firm handle. Whoever praises the Companions of Muhammad is free of hypocrisy. Whoever disparages any of them is an innovator opposing the *Sunna* and the right-acting *Salaf*. It is feared that none of his actions will rise to heaven until he loves them all and his heart is sound."

Qadi 'Iyad also wrote:

He ﷺ said, "Protect me in my Companions and my relations by marriage. Anyone who protects me in them will be protected by Allah in this world and the Next. Anyone who does not protect me in them will be abandoned by Allah. Anyone abandoned by Allah is about to be seized." (Abu Nu'aym and ad-Daylami).

The Prophet ﷺ said, "Whoever protects me in my Companions, I will be his guardian on the Day of Rising." He said, "Whoever protects me in my Companions will come to me at the Basin. Whoever does not protect me in my Companions will not come to me at the Basin and will only see me from a distance." (At-Tabarani).

Malik ibn Anas said, "This Prophet ﷺ taught people the *adab* to which Allah had guided him and which made him a mercy for the worlds. He went out in the darkness of the night to al-Baqi' (the cemetery of Madina), made supplication for the people in the graves and asked forgiveness for them like someone seeing them off on a journey. Allah commanded him to do that and the Prophet commanded people to have love and friendship for them and opposition to anyone who opposes them."

Anas ibn Malik said that the Messenger of Allah ﷺ said, "Allah chose me and He chose my Companions, and He made them my in-laws and made them my helpers. At the end of time, He will bring people who disparage them. Do not become related to them through marriage and do not marry them. Do not have relations with them and do not connect yourselves to them. The curse has alighted upon them."

Qadi 'Iyad also wrote that the Prophet ﷺ said, "Do not curse my Companions. A people will come at the end of time who will curse my Companions. Do not join them and do not join with them and do not marry with them and do not sit in their assemblies. If they are ill, do not visit them."